The ESL Wonder Workbook
Number 1

THIS IS ME

A Book of Lessons and Seatwork
For New Students of English

Elizabeth Claire

With Illustrations by
J. D. Frazier

Original turtle designs
by Yi Lo Cheng

ALTA BOOK CENTER
PUBLISHERS - SAN FRANCISCO

14 ADRIAN COURT
BURLINGAME, CALIFORNIA 94010 USA
415.692.1285 • FAX 415.692.4654
800 ALTA/ESL • 800 ALTA/FAX

Editor: Jackie Flamm
Field Editor: John Heinlein

ALTA BOOK CENTER
PUBLISHERS - SAN FRANCISCO
**14 ADRIAN COURT
BURLINGAME, CALIFORNIA 94010 USA
415.692.1285 • FAX 415.692.4654
800 ALTA/ESL • 800 ALTA/FAX**

ISBN 1-882483-50-2

Acknowledgements

This book owes its existence to the new students and their mainstream teachers at School Number Two in Fort Lee, New Jersey who clamored for simple, do-able ESL activities to insure the productive and effective use of their time. I'd especially like to thank Arlene Dukette, Claire Bufano, Jennie Ambrosio, Jill Ritch, and Chris Theodoropolous for their input during the field development of the materials. I'm also grateful to Hazel Buckwald, Mayra Mateos, Honey Wada, Claudia Poveromo, Sharon Amato, Jean Luppino, Judy Wheeler, Seong Sook Ahn, Lucy Chai, Maria Maier and Joyce Winfield Freedman for ideas and encouragement.

A special thanks to Terri Lehmann for a careful reading of the first draft of the teacher's instructions. I also want to acknowledge the expert editing of Jackie Flamm on the final manuscript, and the contributions by John Heinlein to the readability of the instructions.

Thanks to Mark Lieberman for his example of professional discipline, his editorial assistance, and his homemade soup.

The turtle characters were created in 1986 by Yi Lo Cheng, then age 10. Several of the illustrations are based on the originals by this prize-winning young artist from Taiwan. These have been adapted and artfully executed by Joe Frazier, who is responsible for the design and illustration of the workbook cover and students' pages.

Elizabeth Claire

About the Author

Elizabeth Claire graduated magna cum laude from the City College of New York and was elected into Phi Beta Kappa. She received the Downer Medal of Excellence for Hispanic Studies and was awarded an Experienced Teacher's Fellowship to New York University where she received her Master's Degree in Teaching English as a Second Language. She has taught ESL for the past twenty years to students of all ages and backgrounds. The author of nine other books, she is listed in Who's Who of U.S. Writers, Editors and Poets. She resides in Saddle Brook, New Jersey.

Other works for ESL students and their teachers by Ms. Claire:

ESL Teacher's Activities Kit

ESL Teacher's Holiday Activities Kit

Three Little Words: A, An, and The: A Foreign Student's Guide to English Articles

Hi! English for Children

What's So Funny?: A Foreign Student's Guide to American Humor

Just-a-Minute!: An Oral Language-learning Game

A Foreign Student's Guide to Dangerous English!

TABLE OF CONTENTS

About This Book

THE ESL WONDER WORKBOOKS fill the need for plentiful seatwork to reinforce oral lessons for young beginning students of English. The simple reading, writing, matching, drawing, coloring and other activities insure the productive use of the child's time.

These activities are especially useful for students in mainstream classes who cannot understand or participate in classroom work. Each page of THE ESL WONDER WORKBOOKS focuses on a single, immediately useful language concept with limited vocabulary, leading to easy comprehension and success.

The lessons in WORKBOOK # 1, THIS IS ME, concentrate on the child's own world, identity, and needs, and provide a variety of different reinforcing activities. This keeps the interest level high, and the self-esteem that is often shaky on arrival in a new culture is soon repaired and enhanced. Students will make rapid progress in speaking about themselves, their native countries, their families, their likes and dislikes. They will also learn to understand and respond to classroom instructions in English.

A unique feature of THE ESL WONDER WORKBOOKS is that they can be used by teachers, paraprofessionals, or student aides without special training.

By training English-speaking students to teach the lessons, you can solve the problem of social isolation that often discourages new students. This also addresses the problem of your not having enough time to personally provide all the instruction that your non-English speaking children need.

THIS IS ME contains flexible materials and is sequenced so that most lessons are covered in one, two, or three pages, and do not depend on mastery of previous lessons. Sentence structures are presented for an intuitive learning of grammar; there is no need to explain rules or conduct formal drills. Sight-word reading techniques are incorporated by illustrating each new word and repeating sentence patterns often. You may use the book with students of different ages in a variety of situations:

1. Assign it for supplementary seatwork for newly arrived non-English speaking students in grades two through six.
2. Use it as an introductory text for ESL students in grades one to three, and supplement it with hands-on activities, trips, things to make, songs and games. (See ESL Teacher's Activities Kit, Claire, Prentice Hall Professional Books)
3. You may find that your English-speaking children in grades one and two can also benefit from the additional reading and writing practice. These children may be able to do much of the work on their own.
4. Use it to help learning-disabled students of all ages. The concrete, bite-size lessons and the variety of learning modes allow for the completion and success that enhance students' self-esteem and motivation.

To The Teacher: How to Use This Book

The objectives for each lesson and simple procedures are outlined on each work sheet. These, along with the following suggestions, will help make each lesson a success for both you and your students.

1. GIVE A NEW STUDENT MEANINGFUL WORK TO DO THE FIRST DAY HE OR SHE ARRIVES IN YOUR CLASS. If the student is not able to participate in the class (which could be several hours a day for the first few months), provide for his or her instruction using the ESL WONDER WORKBOOK.

Other materials helpful for the new student:
-- a bilingual dictionary with both English-native language and native
   language-English sections.
-- a picture dictionary
-- classroom textbooks, for students to browse through
-- a battery-operated tape recorder with head phones

2. IF THERE IS NO LANGUAGE INPUT, THERE WILL BE NO INSTRUCTIONAL BENEFITS. There should be interaction with English speakers both before and after the pages are complete. The aim is for the student to mentally practice the new words and sentences as he or she is coloring or writing on a page.

3. HELP THE STUDENT CONNECT WORDS WITH MEANINGS. Speak slowly and clearly; use real objects, actions, facial expressions, and gestures as well as the pictures to insure that the student understands the new words and structures.

4. DO NOT TRANSLATE THE INSTRUCTIONS. The student will easily learn to follow instructions in English. Mime the actions, holding a pencil, crayon, or scissors or whatever is needed and point to the place where the student is to write, draw, cut, or color. Do a sample item as you repeat the instructions.

5. PROVIDE A MODEL FOR THE STUDENT'S RESPONSE. Repeat the words or sentences as often as necessary.

6. DO NOT OVERLOAD. Everything about English is new and strange-sounding at first, and there are no "mental hooks" to hang new words on to. Memory traces for new sounds disappear in a matter of seconds, especially if additional new sounds are immediately presented. Choose a pace that makes it easy for the student to succeed. Remember that students who feel smart learn faster.

7. REVIEW. Each day, review the questions, answers, and vocabulary from work already completed.

8. BE FLEXIBLE. Use the student's reactions and needs to let you know how many pages to assign at a time, how often to review a page, or what additional material to add. Students may complete from one to ten pages a day.

9. GIVE FEEDBACK AND REINFORCEMENT. When the student has finished a page, read it, comment on it, correct it, and ask questions about it. Set standards for careful, neat work. Be honest in your praise and encouragement. Display the student's work in the classroom.

10. TEST. Conduct an informal oral or reading test by asking the questions provided or having the student read the content. When the student has copied words or sentences, give a mini-spelling test of appropriate grade level words. The tests will let you and the student know if more practice is needed.

11. SCHEDULE TIME IN YOUR DAY FOR THE ESL STUDENT. An abbreviated 3-minute session may look like this:
   A. Teach the new words, read the sentences to the student.
   B. Give instructions for completing the pages.
   C. At a later time during the day, correct the pages and interact with the student.

Continued on next on page

Even less time:
- A. One or more classmates teach the new lesson and give instructions to the student.
- B. The classmate corrects the pages and reteaches if necessary. You interact with the student when pages are complete, reinforcing and praising the student's accomplishment.

A 30-minute session with the student may look like this:
- A. Review all the previous pages.
- B. Give a mini spelling test by dictating one sentence or three words.
- C. Check the test in the presence of the student; if more copying work is needed, assign it.
- D. Teach the brief oral lesson for the next page or several pages. Practice with the student.
- E. Give instructions for completing the pages.
- F. Comment on the student's actions, using the present continuous or the past forms of the instructions you gave, i.e., "You are coloring the pictures. Now you are cutting the paper (drawing a line, writing the answer, etc.) Are you finished? You colored this very neatly. I like the pictures you drew. You wrote the wrong word here. You need a capital letter here," and so on.
- G. The student works at his or her seat.
- H. When the work is complete, give feedback. Comment on the coloring, check the answers, have the student read it, and/or ask the student the question or questions that are on the page.

12. KEEP TRACK OF PROGRESS. Use a "three star system." One star on the page indicates that the student understands and responds to the oral English on the page. Two stars mean he or she can read the material. Three stars mean he or she can spell it correctly.

13. PUT THE STUDENT'S LANGUAGE TO USE IN MEANINGFUL SITUATIONS DURING THE DAY. Greet him or her personally, give instructions in English, assign classroom jobs, comment on behavior, ask questions that have yes or no answers or simple one word answers.

14. SHARE THE TASK OF TEACHING WITH OTHER AVAILABLE ENGLISH SPEAKERS. Encourage the entire class to interact with the new student. Pair the student with an English speaking buddy for room chores and errands that will involve contact with others. Train several interested English-speaking students in your class as teachers. This will multiply the instructional time available to the new student and draw him or her more rapidly into the social stream of the class. The enrichment benefits to the tutors is enormous as well, and this role should not be limited to your gifted students. Monitor their teaching to remind them to speak clearly and slowly, and to repeat, praise, and review. Your time with the ESL students can then be a final check after they have had lessons and practice with their peers. Praise both the new student and the "teachers" for their performances.

Teach the terms *objectives* and *procedures* which occur in each set of directions. Be sure your tutors understand the concepts of modeling, demonstrating, and repeating. If the tutor sits on the left of the student, he or she will be able to read the instructions written down the left hand side of the page.

15. KEEP MATERIALS ORGANIZED. Use a three-hole punch on completed pages so the student can keep them in a three-ring binder.

TEACHING VOCABULARY

With the pictures or the real items in front of the student, point to an item, allowing the student to name it if he or she knows it. If not, say the name for it as the student listens. Progress is many times faster when each lesson has a firm foundation in listening comprehension.

Show one item and say its name. Put your finger to your lips to indicate that the student should not repeat the word after you.

Point to a second item and do the same.

Review the first item and then the second item. Go slowly at this point.

Introduce a third item and review the first two. Ask, "Where's the (pen)?" Demonstrate how you want the student to respond by pointing to the pen. Say, "Right!" or "Very good." Continue with "Where's the (pencil)? Where are the (crayons)?" Add two more items and then review all five items. Say the words at random until the student can accurately and without hesitation point to the correct item.

Point to each item for the student to recall and say the names of the items. If the student is not able to, supply the answer for him or her to repeat.

Put the new words into whole-language contexts; use the sentence patterns being taught in the lesson or a pattern previously learned.

Turn to the written form of the words. Point to the words next to each picture and have student say or read them. Model the pronunciation again if necessary.

Cover the pictures so the student may see only the words. Say the words at random for the student to point to.

Say, "Read the words," and listen as the student reads. If the student has difficulty saying a particular sound, slow your pronunciation so the student can see the position of your tongue, lips, and teeth as you make the sound.

Do not frustrate the student by insisting he or she master a difficult sound before moving on; many pronunciation problems of younger students will disappear as they hear more English.

After reviewing several times, and after the student has gained mastery over the vocabulary and conversation suggested by a page, provide additional words, or add comments and new sentences.

FOR PRELITERATE STUDENTS
FOR ASIAN, ARABIC, ISRAELI, GREEK, OR RUSSIAN STUDENTS:

The pages of THIS IS ME are sequenced for students who already know the Roman alphabet. For students who are not yet literate, or whose native language uses a different writing system, the appendix contains practice in letter recognition, matching, writing, and ordering the letters of the alphabet.

You cannot teach phonics without a base of known vocabulary. However, you can foster the student's development of sight-reading ability during the time the oral base of the new language is being built.

After the student has learned some new words orally, point to the words in the sentences as you say them, modeling them for the student to read after you. Write the words on flash cards and drill them separately. Have the student create complete sentences by putting the flash cards in the correct sentence order. Playing the Concentration Game will help with reading and meanings of words.

Include a few pages a day of the letter-recognition pages in the appendix. After Lesson 40, you will have a source of known English words to begin teaching phonics so students will not have to rely on sight reading.

Additional copywork may be necessary at the beginning for students who need practice in forming the letters. Write the words or sentence at the top of the page so the student will have a model to copy. These sheets as well as additional sheets for drawing and notes should be held in the three-ring binder.

Point out capital letters, periods, and other punctuation marks needed.

TIPS FOR PLAYING CONCENTRATION

1. The game can be cut and played as is, but the pieces will have a longer life and blow around less if you copy the page onto cardboard (index stock).

2. Teach the new words for aural recognition.

3. Have the student cut out the words and matching pictures. Point to the pictures. Say, "Pictures." Point to the words. Say, "Words. Shuffle the word cards. I will shuffle the pictures." Demonstrate. Say, "Put the word cards face down on the desk. This is the face of the card. The face goes down. I will lay the picture cards face down on the desk." Demonstrate.

Turn over one picture card, saying the name of the item. Turn over one word card, and read it out loud. Ask, "Are these the same?" If they are the same, say, "Good, these are the same. This is one pair." Put the pair of cards in front on you. Say, "I have one pair. I go again." Repeat. If the cards are not the same, say, "The cards are different. My turn is finished. Now it's your turn."

Say, "Turn over one picture card. Say the name of the picture. Try to find a pair. You want to find the word that says (name of picture). Now turn over a word card." Continue, saying the names or reading the words until all the cards have been matched. Count the number of pairs and say, "I have three pairs. You have nine pairs. You win! You're the winner! Do you want to play again?" Separate the words from the pictures and play again.

Name_____

This is me.

1. Objectives: To understand and respond to the questions "Who is this?" and "What's your name?"; to read and write sentences. Procedure: Point to yourself, saying "My name is _____." Point to the student and ask, "What's your name?" Draw a quick picture of yourself, saying "This is me, _____ (your name). Now draw a picture of you, (student's name)." When the student has completed the picture, ask, "Who is this?" Help the student say, "This is me." Read the questions and sentences and have the student read them after you.

© ELIZABETH CLAIRE 1990

What's your name?

My name is
_____
_ _ _ _ _ _ _ _ _ _ _ _
_____

Name_____

Who are you ?

Write your name.

1. I am _____

2. I am _____

3. _____

4. _____

5. _____

2. Objectives: To understand and respond to the question "Who are you?"; to respond to directions; to practice writing. Procedure: Say, "Who are you?" Help student say, "I am ____." Say, "Write your name here." If the student cannot write his or her name, print the name carefully and neatly on the top line. Read the sentence and have the student read the sentence after you. Say, "Copy the sentence four times."

© ELIZABETH CLAIRE 1990

Name_____

_____

Are you a boy or a girl ?

boy

girl

3. Objectives: To understand and respond to the instruction, "Draw a circle around (the boy)"; to learn the new words: boy, girl. Procedure: Teach the words boy and girl. Point to yourself, saying whatever you are. (If you are an adult, say, woman or man.) Ask, "Are you a boy or a girl? Draw a circle around the _____; " (whatever the student is.) "Write boy (girl) here. Make a big X on the other picture." Demonstrate by making an X in the air. Read the sentence, "I am not (shake your head no) a girl (boy)." Say, "Write the word 'girl' (boy) here." Help the student read the sentences.

© ELIZABETH CLAIRE 1990

I am a_____.

I am not a_____.

Name_____

Page 4

Name_____

Where are you from ?

I'm = I am

I'm from _____

I'm in the United States now.

5. Objectives: To understand and respond to the question, "Where are you from?"; to name and locate one's country and the United States on the world map; to understand and use the contraction, I'm. Procedure: Say, "This is a map. Here is the United States." Point, "I'm from (the United States). Where are you from?" Help the student locate it if necessary. Model, "I'm from ____." for the student to repeat after you. Write the name of the student's country near its location on the map. Say, "Write ____(student's country) here (on the line)."

© ELIZABETH CLAIRE 1990

6. Objectives: To read and write "Where are you from?, I'm from ____." Procedure: Read the sentences to the student, pointing to each word. (Fill in the student's country.) Say, "Read." When the student has read the sentences, say, "Write the sentence here. Copy the sentence three times."

Name_____

Where are you from ?

1. _____

2. _____

3. _____

I'm from _____

1. _____

2. _____

3. _____

© ELIZABETH CLAIRE 1990

Name_____

Flags

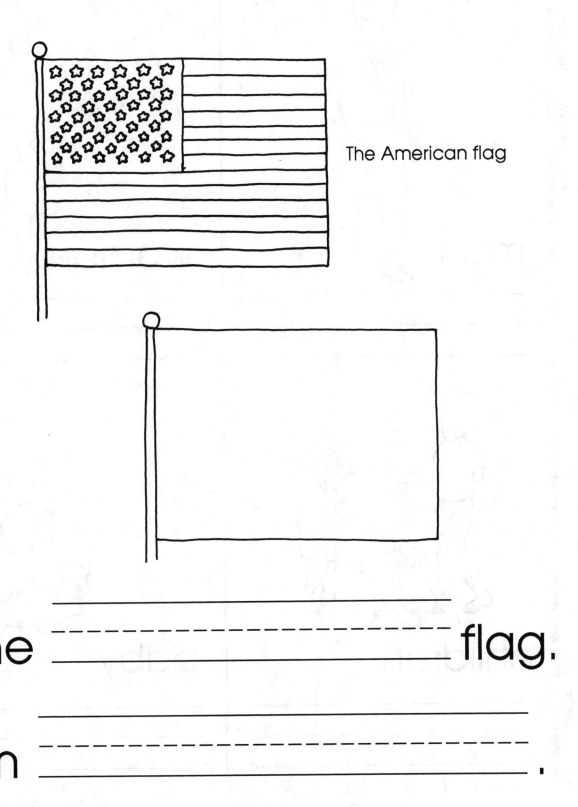

The American flag

The _____ flag.

I'm _____ .

7. Objectives: To state one's nationality; to reinforce sentence patterns. "I'm (Chinese). I'm not (Japanese)." Procedure: Point to the flag and say, "Flag. American flag. This is the flag of the United States of America. Where are you from?" Point to the blank flag. Say, "This is the flag of ___ (student's country) Draw your flag." If necessary, show flag pictures in a dictionary or encyclopedia. If it is too complicated to draw, eliminate this activity.) Say, "I'm from (the United States). I am (American). Are you (American)?" Model the answer. "No, I am not (American). I am _____ (nationality)." Say, "Color the American flag. Color your flag."

© ELIZABETH CLAIRE 1990

8. Objectives: To learn the words man, woman, children, and baby; to reinforce the directions. "Copy the words." Procedure: Teach the new words. Read the words and then have the student read the words. Say, "Copy the words here."

© ELIZABETH CLAIRE 1990

people

man

woman

children

baby

Draw a picture of your teacher.

This is my teacher.

Who is your teacher ?

_____

My teacher is_____.

My teacher is ☐ a man.
☐ a woman.

9. Objective: To learn the classroom teacher's name and to respond to the question, "Who is your teacher?" Procedure: Point to the teacher if she or he is in the room, (or yourself, if you are the teacher) and say, "Teacher. That is your (our) teacher. Her (his) name is _____. (I am your teacher. My name is _____.) Draw a picture of your teacher." When completed, read the sentences on the page for the student to read after you. Write the teacher's name on a separate sheet of paper, point to the line, and say, "Write the teacher's name here. Is the teacher (Am I) a man or a woman? Make a check here." Demonstrate. Point to the sentences, and say, "Read."
© ELIZABETH CLAIRE 1990

Name_____

Good morning.

Good morning.

a.m.

Good afternoon.

Good afternoon.

p.m.

10. Objectives: To understand and respond to greetings; to learn the new words: sun, morning, noon, afternoon, turtle. Procedure: Point to the sun. Say, "Here is the sun. It's morning. We say, 'Good morning.' in the morning." Point to the second picture. Say, "It's noon." Point to the sun in the picture. Say, "It's afternoon. We say, 'Good afternoon.' in the afternoon." Point to the turtles. Say, "These are turtles. The turtles are saying 'Good morning.' Can you say that?" Point to the second picture. "These turtles are saying 'good afternoon.'"

© ELIZABETH CLAIRE 1990

Page 10

Copy the words.

Good morning.

1. _____

2. _____

3. _____

Good afternoon.

1. _____

2. _____

3. _____

11. Objectives: To practice reading and copying the phrases good morning and good afternoon; to reinforce instructions "Copy the words (three) times." Procedure: Read the phrases, modelling them for the student to read after you. Say, "Copy 'good morning' three times." Point to each numbered line and say, "Write 'good morning' here, write 'good morning' here; and write 'good morning' here. Copy 'good afternoon' three times."

© ELIZABETH CLAIRE 1990

How are you ?

1. How are you ?

2. I'm fine, thank you.

3. How are you ?

4. Not so good.

How are you ?

_____

_ (fine/not so good) here.

12. Objective: To understand and respond to the question, "How are you?" Procedure: Smile, throw your chest out, flex your muscles to demonstrate health and vigor; point to yourself and say, "I'm fine." Point to the student and say, "How are you? Fine? Or are you not so good?" Frown, cough, limp, hold your hand over your head, speak with a scratchy voice, and so on. Then demonstrate good health again and say, "I'm fine." If student says, "I'm fine," add "Thank you." Ask the question again for the student to say, "I'm fine, thank you." Read the conversation on the page for the student to read after you. Say, "How are you?" Listen to the student's answer and say, "Write _____ fine, thank you." Read the conversation on the page for the student to read after you. Say, "How are you?" Listen to the student's answer and say, "Write good) here.

Copy the words.

How are you ?

1. _____

2. _____

3. _____

I'm fine, thank you.

I'm =
I am

1. _____

2. _____

3. _____

13. Objectives: To practice reading and copying; to learn the contraction, I'm. Procedure: Point to the box where the contraction is shown. Say, "I'm is the same as I am. I am fine. I'm fine. Same thing. This is an apostrophe." Point to the apostrophe. "Look, there's no letter a." Point to "How are you?" Say, "This is a question." Point to "I'm fine, thank you." Say, "This is an answer." Say, "Copy the question three times here." Point to the appropriate lines. "Copy the answer three times here."

Name_____

Things in School

Color the pictures. Copy the words.

pencil

_____

— — — — — — — — — —

_____

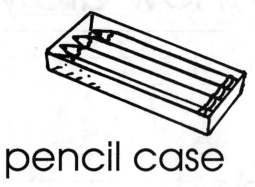

pencil case

_____

— — — — — — — — — —

_____

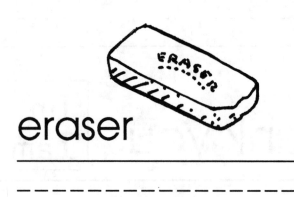

eraser

_____

— — — — — — — — — —

_____

paper

_____

— — — — — — — — — —

_____

book

_____

— — — — — — — — — —

_____

crayons

_____

— — — — — — — — — —

_____

14. Objective: To learn the names of objects in school. Procedure: Teach the new words using real objects. Have the student point to the objects and read the words under each picture. Say, "Color the picture." Give the student a sheet of paper, and say, "Copy the words five times each." © ELIZABETH CLAIRE 1990

Things in School -- Match

Draw a line from the word to the picture.
Write the word.

words   pictures

1. paper

_____

- - - - - - - - - - - - - - - - - - -

_____

2. book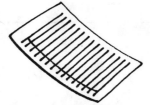

_____

- - - - - - - - - - - - - - - - - - -

_____

3. pencil

_____

- - - - - - - - - - - - - - - - - - -

_____

4. crayons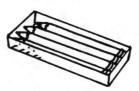

_____

- - - - - - - - - - - - - - - - - - -

_____

5. eraser

_____

- - - - - - - - - - - - - - - - - - -

_____

6. pencil case

- - - - - - - - - - - - - - - - - - -

_____

15. Objectives: To reinforce reading and writing of school objects; to understand and follow the direction, "Draw a line from ___ to ___." Procedure: Read the title of the page; have the student read after you. Point to the list of words, and say, "Words. Read the words." Point to the pictures and say, "Pictures. What is this picture?" Have the student say the names of the items in the pictures. Say "Draw a line." Demonstrate on another sheet of paper. Say, "Draw a line from the word (point to the words) to the picture (point to the picture). Then write the word here."

© ELIZABETH CLAIRE 1990

More Things in School

Color the pictures. Copy the words.

desk

_____

- - - - - - - - - - - - -

_____

chair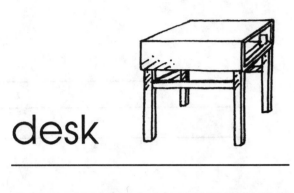

_____

- - - - - - - - - - - - -

_____

blackboard

_____

- - - - - - - - - - - - -

_____

chalk

_____

- - - - - - - - - - - - -

_____

clock

_____

- - - - - - - - - - - - -

_____

ruler

_____

- - - - - - - - - - - - -

_____

16. Objective: To learn the names of more school objects. Procedure: Teach the words using real objects. Review items from the previous lesson. Have the student point to the objects and read the words under each picture. Say, "Copy the words five times each." This is done on a separate sheet of paper.

© ELIZABETH CLAIRE 1990

Name_____

More Things in School -- Match

Draw a line from the word to the picture.
Write the word.

words   pictures

1. chair   _____
                                        - - - - - - - - -

2. clock   - - - - - - - - -

3. desk   - - - - - - - - -
                                        _____

4. ruler      - - - - - - - - -

5. blackboard    - - - - - - - - -
                                        _____

6. chalk      _____
                                        - - - - - - - - -

17. Objectives: To reinforce reading and writing of words for school objects; to reinforce following the direction. "Draw a line from __ to __." Procedure: Read the title of the page; have the student read after you. Point to the list of words and say, "Words." Point to the pictures and say, "Pictures." Say, "Read the words." The student reads. Point to each picture and say, "What's this?" Say, "Draw a line from the word to the picture." Demonstrate if necessary.

© ELIZABETH CLAIRE 1990

22. Objective: To learn the names of other items in the classroom. e.g., picture, scissors, paste, computer, markers, compass, sink, heater, bulletin board, and so on.
Procedure: Read the title. Point to the picture of the notebook. Say, "This is a notebook. Draw a picture of other things in school." Point to several objects as examples, but allow
student to choose what he or she will draw. As the student completes the pictures, say the names of the objects he or she has drawn. Write the word for each object in the box
it is drawn in. Say, "Copy these words (three) times each."

Name _____

Other Things in School

Draw pictures of other things in school.
Write the words.

notebook

© ELIZABETH CLAIRE 1990

Page 18

Name_____

Color the pictures. Cut out the pictures.

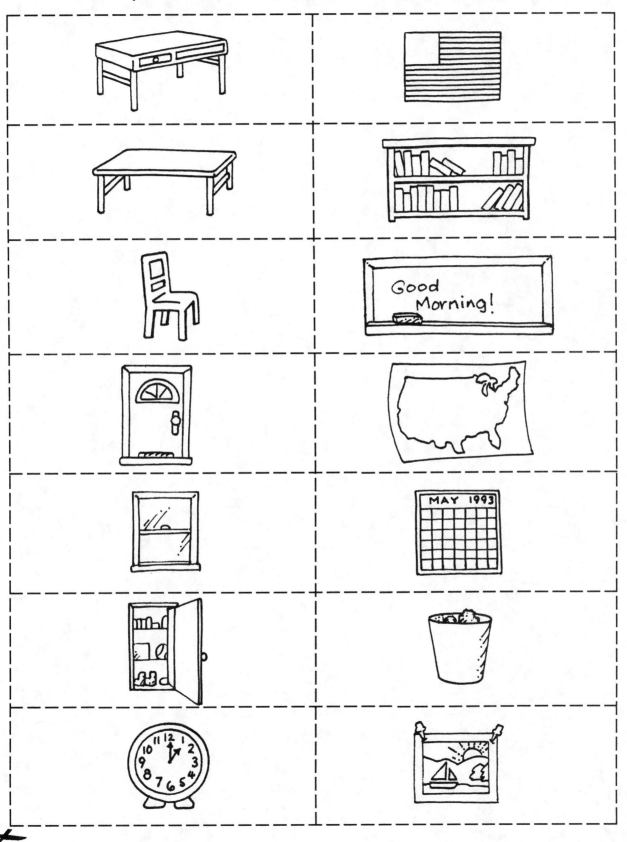

Good Morning!

MAY 1993

18 and 20. Objective: To reinforce reading and spelling of names of objects in the classroom. Procedure: Have the student read the words and say the names of the pictures.

Page 19

Name_____

Name_____

Cut out the words.

desk	flag
table	bookshelf
chair	blackboard
door	map
window	calendar
closet	waste basket
clock	picture

Page 21

Name_____

This is my classroom.

23. Objective: To review the names of objects in the classroom. Procedure: Say, "This is our classroom.". Point to various items around the room. Say, "What can you see in the classroom.". Acknowledge everything that the student can name and teach the names of other items. Say, "Draw a picture of the classroom. Write the names of the things that you draw."

© ELIZABETH CLAIRE 1990

Write the names of the things in the picture.

Name_____

Kids in My Class

_____   _____
- - - - - - - - - - - - -   - - - - - - - - - - - - -
_____   _____

_____   _____
- - - - - - - - - - - - -   - - - - - - - - - - - - -
_____   _____

_____   _____
- - - - - - - - - - - - -   - - - - - - - - - - - - -
_____   _____

_____   _____
- - - - - - - - - - - - -   - - - - - - - - - - - - -
_____   _____

_____   _____
- - - - - - - - - - - - -   - - - - - - - - - - - - -

More kids in my class

24 and 25. Objective: To learn the names of the students in the class. Procedure: Point to students in the class and teach their names a few at a time. Ask, "What's his (her) name?" Help the student with pronunciation. Dictate the letters in the classmates' names as the student writes the names. Label the columns Row one, row two, and so on, if the classroom is in rows, or, table one, and so on. Optional: Have the student go to each classmate during a break and ask, "What's your name? Write your name here."

© ELIZABETH CLAIRE 1990

How many ?

0 1 2 3 4 5

_____ cats

_____ books

_____ cakes

_____ boys

_____ girl

_____ telephones

How many ?

6 7 8 9 10

27. Objectives: To learn the numbers 6-10; to practice numbers with plural nouns. Procedure: Teach the numbers. Say, "Count from one to ten." Point to each picture and have the student say the name of the items. Say "Count the flags. (Seven) Write the number seven here. Good. Seven flags. Count the things in each picture and write the number." When the student is finished, have her or him read the phrases to you. Say, "Color the pictures."

© ELIZABETH CLAIRE 1990

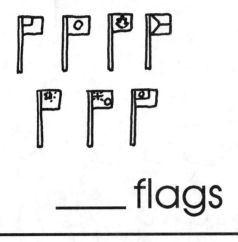

___ flags

___ doors

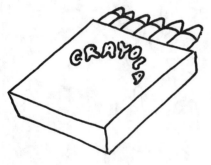

___ crayons

___ pencils

___ children

___ cups

Name_____

Draw candles on the cake to show how old you are.

How old are you ?

candles

cake

1 2 3 4 5 6 7 8 9 10
11 12 13 14 15

I'm ____ years old.

28. Objectives: To understand and answer the question "How old are you?"; to learn the numbers 11-15; to learn new words: cake, candles, birthday. Procedure: Sing the song "Happy Birthday." Invite the student to sing along in his or her own language. Ask, "How old are you?" Point to the candles on the cake. "One, two, three, four. Are you four years old?" Model the sentence "I'm (eight) years old." Say, "Write (eight) here." Point to the blank. Point to the cake, then the candles. Say, "This is a birthday cake. These are candles. How many candles are there? (Four) Draw more candles to show how old you are." Demonstrate. Teach the numbers 11-15. Count from 1 to 15. Read the sentences and have the student read after you.

© ELIZABETH CLAIRE 1990

Name_____

Copy the sentences below.

How old are you ?

I'm____years old.

| I'm =
| I am |

----

29. Objective: To read and write "How are you?; to reinforce the contraction I'm; to write sentences using question marks, periods, and apostrophes. Procedure: Point to the sentences and say, "Read the sentences." Point to the contraction I'm in the box. Say, "I'm. I'm is the same as I am." Point to the apostrophe. Say, "This is an apostrophe. There is no 'a' here. The apostrophe shows that a letter is missing. I'm is one word." Point to I am. Say, "I am is two words. I'm and I am are the same. Read the sentences. Copy the sentences four times each."
© ELIZABETH CLAIRE 1990

Page 29

Name_____

My Telephone

What is your telephone number ?

My telephone number

is _____ .

30. Objectives: To learn one's telephone number; to understand and respond to the question, "What's your telephone number?" Procedure: Point to the telephone and say, "Telephone. Do you have a telephone? What's your telephone number?" If the student doesn't know the number, look it up in his or her class records, or write a reminder for him or her to bring the number to school the next day. Have the student practice saying his or her telephone number until it is learned. Say, "Write your telephone number here." Read the words and sentences on the page. Say, "Copy the sentences three times each." (On a separate sheet of paper.) © ELIZABETH CLAIRE 1990

Page 30

Name_____

RING!
RING!

1. Hello.
2. This is Tom.

1. _____

2. _____

3. Hi Tom.
4. This is Betty.

3. _____

4. _____

5. Goodbye.

5. _____

Page 31

Numbers

Copy the number words 3 times each.

32 and 33. Objective: To read the words for the numbers one through ten. Procedure: Teach the words and check the student's ability to read them. Then point to the line. Say, "Copy the number words three times each."

one

two

three

four

five

six

© ELIZABETH CLAIRE 1990

Name_____

Numbers, 2

Copy the number words 3 times each.

seven

_____
- - - - - - - - - -
_____
- - - - - - - - - -
_____
- - - - - - - - - -
_____

eight

_____
- - - - - - - - - -
_____
- - - - - - - - - -
_____
- - - - - - - - - -
_____

nine

_____
- - - - - - - - - -
_____
- - - - - - - - - -
_____
- - - - - - - - - -
_____

ten

_____
- - - - - - - - - -
_____
_____
- - - - - - - - - -
_____
_____
- - - - - - - - - -
_____

zero

_____
- - - - - - - - - -
_____
_____
- - - - - - - - - -
_____
_____
- - - - - - - - - -
_____

© ELIZABETH CLAIRE 1990

Numbers, Match

Match.

1	two	◇ ◇ ◇
2	one	☐ ☐
3	three	● ● ● ●
4	five	△
5	four	○ ○ ○ ○ ○

6	eight	☐☐☐☐ ☐☐☐☐
7	six	●●●● ●●●● ●
8	nine	△△△△ △△
9	ten	✳✳✳✳ ✳✳✳
10	seven	_____
0	zero	●●●● ●●●● ●●

34. Objective: To reinforce and check reading of number words. Procedure: Point to the numbers and say, "Numbers." Point to the number words and say, "Words." Point to the small shapes and say, "Things." Say, "Draw a line from the number to the word. Then draw a line from the word to the things that show how many." Be sure to demonstrate.

© ELIZABETH CLAIRE 1990

Name_____

What is It ?
Draw a line from number one to number ten.

• three

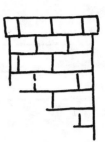

two • ————————————————————— • four

eight
•

seven
•

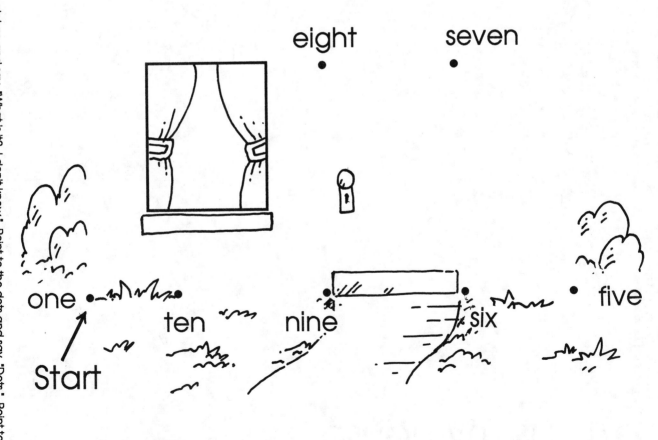

one •

Start

ten

nine

six

five

It's a _____ .

Name_____

Where do you live ?

I live at

_____

- -

_____

Draw a picture of your house.

This is my house.

36. Objective: To tell one's street address. Procedure: Find out the student's address before the lesson. Ask "Where do you live?" Model the answer for the student and have him or her repeat it after you several times as clearly as possible. Draw a sketch of your house and say, "This is my house." Draw a picture of your house." When the drawing is complete, admire the house. Point to the things the student has drawn and tell the names of them as the student repeats after you. For example: door, window, roof, grass, tree, chimney, first floor, second floor, and so on. Write the words on the picture for the student to read. The student may copy the words on another sheet of paper.

Name_____

37. Objectives: To learn that many words for things end in s to show more than one; to pronounce final s. Procedure: Point to the girl and say, "One girl." Point to the three girls and say, "Three girls." Continue with each item. Say, "Read" as you point to each item. Model the final s clearly for the student. Say, "What letter is here? (S) This s means 'more than one.' Color the pictures. Copy the words."

One

girl

cat

eye

flag

More than one

girls

cats

eyes

flags

© ELIZABETH CLAIRE 1990

What is it ?

38. Objectives: To learn the numbers 16 to 21; to count to 29. Procedure: Point to the numbered dots and say, "What is it? I don't know. Draw a line from number one to two. Say the numbers." Listen as student says each number. Teach the numbers not known. When complete, say, "What is it? It's a bird. Write bird here: B,I,R,D." Have the student continue to count to 29.

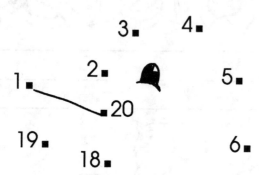

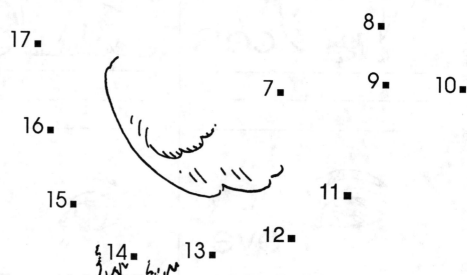

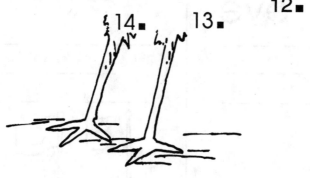

3.■   4.■

2.■   5.■

1   20.■

19.■   6.■

18.■

17.■   8.■

16.■   9.■   10.■

7.■

15.■   11.■

12.■

14.■   13.■

It's a _____

© ELIZABETH CLAIRE 1990

Name_____

_____

Practice with numbers.

a. 6   2   5   8   1

b. 4   3   0   9   7

c. 10   12   11   15   14

d. 16   18   20   17   19

e. 23   21   22   26   24

f. six ____   four ____   two ____

g. nine ____ five ____   one ____

h. ten ____ zero ____   three ____

i. seven ____   eight ____

39. Objective: To reinforce comprehension, speaking and reading of the numbers 0-29. Procedure: Say, "Say the numbers in row a, row b, and so on." "Write the number next to the word in row f." and so on. On a separate sheet of paper, dictate numbers at random for the student to write.

© ELIZABETH CLAIRE 1990

40. Objective: To practice the sentence pattern, "I have (six) (pens)." Procedure: Put several of the student's books, crayons, pencils, and other objects on the student's desk. Put a number of similar objects on your desk. Point to the student's objects and count. "One, two, three books." You have three books." Then count the books on your desk. "One, two. I have two books." Do this for each item. Say, "What do I have?" Help student say, "You have (three) (pencils)." Say, "What do you have?" Student answers. Then read the directions as you point to the sentences. Say, "Count your pencils. Write the number here." When completed, say, "Read your sentences."

At My Desk

1. I have _____ pencils.

2. I have _____ pens.

3. I have _____ crayons.

4. I have _____ books.

5. I have _____ _____ .

6. I _____ _____ _____ .

7. _____ _____ _____ .

© ELIZABETH CLAIRE 1990

41. Objective: To use polite forms for requesting things. Procedure: Gather some items on the student's desk. Teach or review the names of the items. Say, "May I have a (book) please?" If the student does not know what to do, take his or her hand, fold the fingers around the object, and bring the hand to your hand. Take the object and say, "Thank you!" Repeat with each item on the desk. When all the items are in front of you, hold up (a pen) and indicate that the student is to request it from you, saying, "May I have a _____, please?" Remind the student to say, "Thank you." Have the student request all of the items on the desk. Read the sentences and have the student read after you.

© ELIZABETH CLAIRE 1990

Page 41

Ask for Something
Copy:

1. May I have a pen, please?

2. Thank you.

3. You're welcome.

42. Objective: To practice writing using capital letters, periods, commas, apostrophes and question marks. Procedure: Read the title and the directions to the student. Say, "Copy the sentences two times each." When complete, check carefully for letter formation and the use of punctuation marks. If any are missing, point to the place, and say, "Write a (comma) here." © ELIZABETH CLAIRE 1990

The Clown

43. Objective: To learn the words for parts of the face. Procedure: Teach the names of each part of your face as you point to it. Review. Indicate your entire face, and say, "Face." Point to the clown and say, "This is a clown. This is her face. I'll read the words and you read after me." Read the directions to the student. When the student has completed coloring the clown, review the words and comment on the coloring. Add other parts of the face when reviewing this page. E.g., chin, cheek, eyebrow, and so on.

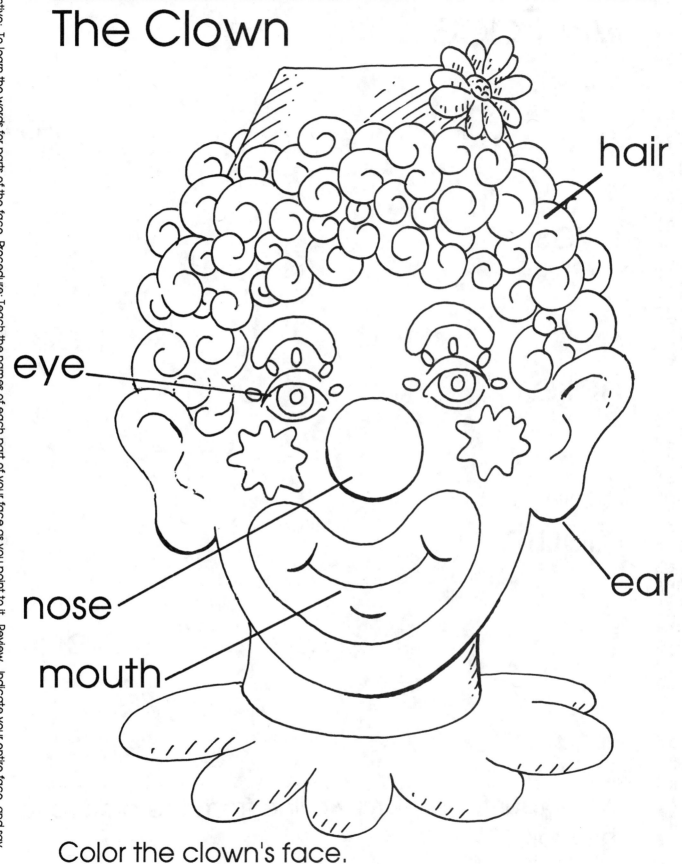

hair

eye

ear

nose

mouth

Color the clown's face.

Page 43

My Face

hair

eyes

ear

nose

mouth

neck

Draw your face. Draw a line from the picture to the word.

44. Objective: To reinforce words for parts of the face. Procedure: Use a small mirror if available. Draw your own face, and label the parts. Say: "Look in the mirror. Draw your face. Draw a line from the word to the part of your face." When completed, comment on the drawing. Teach words for any items the student has drawn: glasses, eyelashes, and so on. Label these items. The student may write the words several times each in his or her notebook for additional practice.

© ELIZABETH CLAIRE 1990

Name_____

What's Missing?

Draw the part that is missing.
Write the word.

45. Objectives: To reinforce and practice writing words for parts of the face; to understand and respond to the question. "What's Missing?" Point to the first picture. Say, "What's missing? An eye is missing. There is only one eye. Draw an eye in the face. Write the word eye here. Look at the other faces. What's missing? Draw the part of the face that is missing. Write the word for the parts that are missing." When complete, comment on the drawing and check the words and spelling. Procedure: Read the title, "What's Missing?"

© ELIZABETH CLAIRE 1990

Page 45

It is unlawful to reproduce this page without express written permission from the Publisher.

46. Objective: To learn the names of parts of the body. Procedure: Teach the words as you point to your own head, neck, shoulders, and so on. Gesture to indicate your entire body and say, "Body." Read the words for the body parts as the student reads after you. Then student reads alone. Say, "Color the picture."

© ELIZABETH CLAIRE 1990

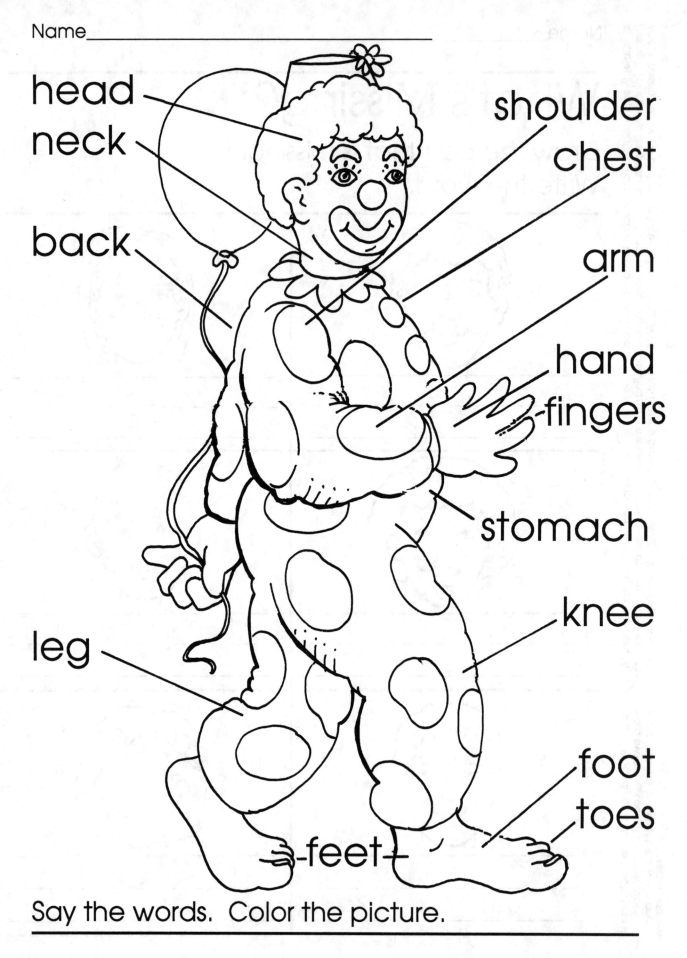

head
neck

shoulder
chest

back

arm

hand
fingers

stomach

knee

leg

foot
toes

feet

Say the words. Color the picture.

Page 46

Name_____

My Body

Draw your body. Draw a line from the picture to the word.

head
neck
shoulder

arm
chest

hand
fingers

stomach

leg

knee

foot
toes

feet

fingers

right

Put your hands on the paper. Draw your hands.

thumbs

| My Hands |

fingers

left

© ELIZABETH CLAIRE 1990

48. Objective: To learn the words for fingers, thumbs; left and right. Procedure: Say "Place your hands on this paper. Place your right hand here, and your left hand here." Demonstrate. Point to the student's right hand and say, "This is your right hand." Point to the student's left hand and say, "This is your left hand. These are your fingers. These are your thumbs. Draw a picture of your hand. Trace your hand." (You will have to trace one of the hands for the student as it is difficult to trace the writing hand with the other hand.) Label the words. Add items the student has drawn such as ring, watch, bracelet.

Page 48

Name_____

How Many Do You Have ?

1	2	10
one	two	ten

1. I have <u>two</u> eyes.

2. I have ____ nose.

3. I have ____ mouth.

4. I have ____ neck.

5. I have ____ arms

6. I _____ hands.

7. _____ fingers.

8. _____ legs.

9. _____ feet.

10. _____ toes.

A Big Family

50. Objectives: To share information about your families; to learn the names for people in a family. Procedure: Show photos of members of your family or draw a picture of your family. Say, "This is my (mother/sister/husband/son/ and so on)." Point to the picture. Say the names of the people in the family as the student reads after you. You may ask as you point to each person in the picture, "Do you have a (sister?)" or "How many (grandmothers) do you have?"

© ELIZABETH CLAIRE 1990

Color the picture.   Say the names.

51. Objective: To continue sharing information about your families. Procedure: Say, "Draw a picture of your family here in the United States." When complete, point to each person and ask, "Who is this?" Help the student label the people in the picture. Read the sentence at the bottom of the page, "I live with my ___." Say, "Write the people in your family here." Ask questions about the people in the picture: "What's your brother's name? How old is he?" And so on. Tell the student about your family.

Name_____

My Family

Draw the people in your family here.
Write the names.

I live with my_____

_____

_____

_____

© ELIZABETH CLAIRE 1990

Name_____
_____

My Family II

Draw the people in your family in your country.
Write the names.

My _____
_ _
_____

_____
live in _____
_ .

Name_____

My School

What school do you go to ?

I go to _____

This is my school.

Name_____

What grade are you in ?

I am in

kindergarten

first grade

second grade

third grade

fourth grade

fifth grade

sixth grade

middle school / junior high

high school

Name_____

My School

1. I go to _____

2. I go to _____

3. I _____

4. I am in _____ grade.

5. I am in _____

6. I _____

Name_____

Go to school.

Draw a line from home to school.

START

HOME

PARK

STOP

HOSPITAL

SCHOOL

Page 56

Name_____

In My School, I
Color the picture. Copy the words.

classroom

_____

- - - - - - - - - - - - - -

_____

hall

_____

- - - - - - - - - - - - - -

_____

stairs

_____

- - - - - - - - - - - - - -

_____

office

_____

- - - - - - - - - - - - - -

_____

57 and 58 Objective: To learn the names of the various places in the school. Procedure: Take the student on a tour of the school. Name the special rooms such as classroom, bathroom, lunch room, gym, office, nurse's office, library, music room, computer room, auditorium. Read the words under the pictures and have the student read after you. Say, "Copy the names of these places. Color the pictures."

© ELIZABETH CLAIRE 1990

Name_____

In My School, II
Color the picture. Copy the words.

library

_____
- - - - - - - - - - -
_____

gym

_____
- - - - - - - - - - -
_____

nurse's office

_____
- - - - - - - - - - -
_____

auditorium

_____
- - - - - - - - - - -
_____

57 and 58 Objective: To learn the names of the various places in the school. Procedure: Take the student on a tour of the school. Name the special rooms such as classroom, bathroom, lunch room, gym, office, nurse's office, library, music room, computer room, auditorium. Read the words under the pictures and have the student read after you. Say, "Copy the names of these places. Color the pictures."

© ELIZABETH CLAIRE 1990

Name_____

Copy the name of your town and state.

My town is

1.

2.

3.

My state is

1.

2.

3.

59. Objective: To name the town or city and state in which you live. Procedure: Ask, "Where do you live?" The student gives the number and street. Then add, "(name of town, name of state)." Let the student practice several times. Write the name of the town and state in appropriate places. Say, "Copy (name of town) and (name of state) three times."

© ELIZABETH CLAIRE 1990

60. Objectives: To reinforce ability to state one's address; to learn to address an envelope; to learn new words: address, envelope, stamp, first name, last name, top line, zip code. Procedure: Show an envelope that has been addressed to you or make up an envelope with a fictitious name and address. Say, "This is an envelope. Here is the address. Here is (my) first name and (my) last name. This is the number of (my) house. This is the name of (my) street. This is the town and state. This number is the zip code. What's your address?" Help student answer. Say, "Write your address here." When it is completed, check it. Give the student a blank envelope. Make a dot to show the student where to begin writing the address. Write a short note to the student, place it in the envelope. Place a stamp in the correct corner and mail it. © ELIZABETH CLAIRE 1990

STAMP

Address —

First Name, Last Name
Number, Street
Town, State, Zip Code
U. S. A.

A letter to me

STAMP

Name_____

A letter to my teacher

_____

_____

_____

Return Address

STAMP

_____

_____

_____

A letter to my friend

_____

_____

_____

STAMP

_____

_____

_____

Mail the letter.

US MAIL

Page 61

61. Objective: To continue learning to address an envelope, including the return address. Procedure: Say, "Let's write an envelope to the teacher (me). Write my (the teacher's) name here on the top line. Write the name of the school here on the second line. Write the number and street on the third line. Write the town and the state and the zip code on the fourth line. Now in this corner, (point to upper left) you write your address. To address the next envelope, the student will have to ask a classmate for his or her name and address. When the samples are complete, give the student two envelopes on which to copy the addresses.

© ELIZABETH CLAIRE 1990

Today, I am...

1. happy

2. sad

3. angry

4. sleepy

5. afraid

62. Objective: To learn vocabulary for expressing emotions. Procedure: Use facial expressions and gestures as you say, I'm (happy.) Invite the student to copy your expressions as he or she says the sentences after you. Point to the first blank face. Say, "This person is happy. Draw a happy face," and so on. Demonstrate the facial expression so the student understands the emotion for each drawing. Then say, "Say a sentence for each picture. (He's happy; She's sad.) Write the sentences on another sheet of paper." For the last picture on the page, let the student draw another emotion. Try to guess it from his or her facial expression and write the word for it under the picture. Possibilities are: worried, bored, asleep, surprised, hungry, thirsty, furious. © ELIZABETH CLAIRE 1990

Page 62

This makes me:
happy, sad, afraid, angry

1. _____

2. _____

3. _____

4. _____

5. _____

6. _____

7. _____

8. _____

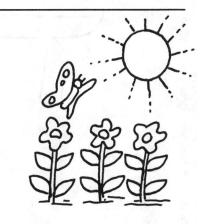

9. _____

Name_____

64. Objectives: To express hunger; to learn words for nutritious foods. Procedure: Collect pictures of some common foods like eggs, bread, soup, rice, beans, vegetables, fruit, cereal, meat, sandwiches. Teach a small number of words at a time, review them, and teach two or three more. Read the title and the sentences. The student reads after you. Name the foods on the table; the student repeats after you. Make sentences with "Let's eat _____." Use the words in the picture. Say, "Color the picture." © ELIZABETH CLAIRE 1990

Food

spaghetti
rice
soup
salad
beans
corn
bread
sandwiches
fruit
vegetables
peas
potato
beets
carrots
green beans

I'm hungry.
Let's eat.

Color the picture.

Page 64

Desk-top Match Game

banana	carrot
orange	peas
apple	potato
grapes	corn
strawberries	rice
sandwich	chicken

Cut out the words. ✂

65 and 67. Objectives: To read and reinforce words for foods; to learn a simple game and the language needed to play it. Procedure: If possible, photocopy pages 65 and 67 onto cardboard or index stock. Teach or review the vocabulary. Supply scissors and say, "We are going to play a game." Cut out the cards. Play Concentration as described on page ix. © ELIZABETH CLAIRE 1990

Name_____

Color the pictures. Cut out the pictures.

65 and 67. Objectives: To read and reinforce words for foods; to learn a simple game and the language needed to play it. Procedure: If possible, photocopy pages 65 and 67 onto cardboard or index stock. Teach or review the vocabulary. Supply scissors and say, "We are going to play a game. Cut out the cards." Play Concentration as described on page Ix.

© ELIZABETH CLAIRE 1990

Name_____

Name_____

I like to eat

69. Objective: To express food likes and learn the names of additional foods. Procedure: Say, "I like to eat _____," and tell something you like to eat, showing that you like it. Ask, "What do you like to eat? Draw pictures of things you like to eat." When complete, tell the student the English words for the pictures drawn. The student may copy the words on a separate sheet of paper. Optional: supply the student with a magazine with food pictures that may be cut and pasted onto the student's page.　© ELIZABETH CLAIRE 1990

70. Objective: To express thirst; to learn words for beverages; to request a drink. Procedure: Teach the new words. Read the sentences as the student listens. Read the name of each drink as you point to it and the student reads after you. Say, "May I have a drink, please? May I have milk please? May I have lemonade please?" The student should point to the beverage you are requesting. Then point to each picture and have the student request that beverage.

I'm thirsty.

May I have
a drink, please ?

milk

water

orange
juice

tomato
juice

soda

coffee

tea

lemonade

71. Objective: To read and write sentences requesting beverages; to reinforce beverage words. Procedure: Say, "Write the sentence, 'May I have a drink please?'" The student writes, "Now write 'May I have milk, please?' Write 'May I have' (something else), please?' Write 6 different sentences."
© ELIZABETH CLAIRE 1990

Name_____

_____

1. May I have <u>milk</u> please ?

2. May I have_____ please ?

3. _____

4. _____

5. _____

6. _____

7. _____

Name_____

I like to play

72. Objectives: To talk about games; to express knowledge of games; ability to play and preferences in games; to learn new words: soccer, hopscotch, board games, baseball. Procedure: Teach the names of the four games, using the pictures. Ask, "Do you like to play (soccer)?" Have the student check yes or no. Help the student say, "I like to play (hopscotch); I (don't) like to play (baseball)." Say, "Copy the words. Color the pictures. Write sentences on another sheet of paper."

soccer ☐ yes ☐ no

_____
- - - - - - - - - - - - -
_____

hopscotch ☐ yes ☐ no

_____
- - - - - - - - - - - - -
_____

board games ☐ yes ☐ no

_____
- - - - - - - - - - - - -
_____

baseball ☐ yes ☐ no

_____
- - - - - - - - - - - - -
_____

© ELIZABETH CLAIRE 1990

Name_____

I like to play

_____   _____
- - - - - - - - - - - - - - -   - - - - - - - - - - - - - - -
_____   _____

_____   _____
- - - - - - - - - - - - - - -   - - - - - - - - - - - - - - -
_____   _____

73. Objective: To continue to talk about games and express preferences in games. Procedure: Say, "Draw pictures of the games you like to play." When the student has completed the pictures, label them. Have the student copy the words and make sentences with, "I like to play _____."

© ELIZABETH CLAIRE 1990

Name_____

74. Objective: To say greetings and farewells for the evening. Procedure: Point to the sun in the picture. Say, "Sun. The sun is going down. It's evening. We say, 'Good evening' in the evening." Repeat 'Good evening' until the student can say it. Then point to the second picture. Say, "The turtle is going home. He says 'Good night.'" Stand up and go to bed.
© ELIZABETH CLAIRE 1990

Page 74

Copy the words.

Good evening.

_____
- -
_____

_____
- -
_____

_____
- -
_____

Good night.

_____
- -
_____

_____
- -
_____

_____
- -
_____

75. Objective: To practice copying and spelling "Good evening" and "Good night." Procedure: Point to the words and say, "Read these words." Model the words if necessary. Say, "Copy the words three times each." © ELIZABETH CLAIRE 1990

All About Me

My name is _____

_____.

I am a _____. (boy, girl)

I am _____ years old. I come

from_____.

I go to _____

_____. I am

in _____ grade.   My teacher

is _____ _____.

Name_____

_____

All About Me

I have _____ brothers and

_____ sisters.   I live with

my _____

at _____ _____
     number   name of street

in_____
     town / city

_____, USA.
state

I like to play _____

and _____.

Name_____

Draw a circle around the word that is the same as the first word.

1. boy   bed   buy   boy   toy

2. man   map   man   fan   men

3. woman   what   walk   who   woman

4. baby   body   boy   bad   baby

5. this   thing   his   this   that

6. my   me   by   mine   my

7. girl   good   girl   game   get

8. not   net   no   not   now

9. you   you   your   yes   our

10. from   frog   fire   flag   from

Page 78

Name_____

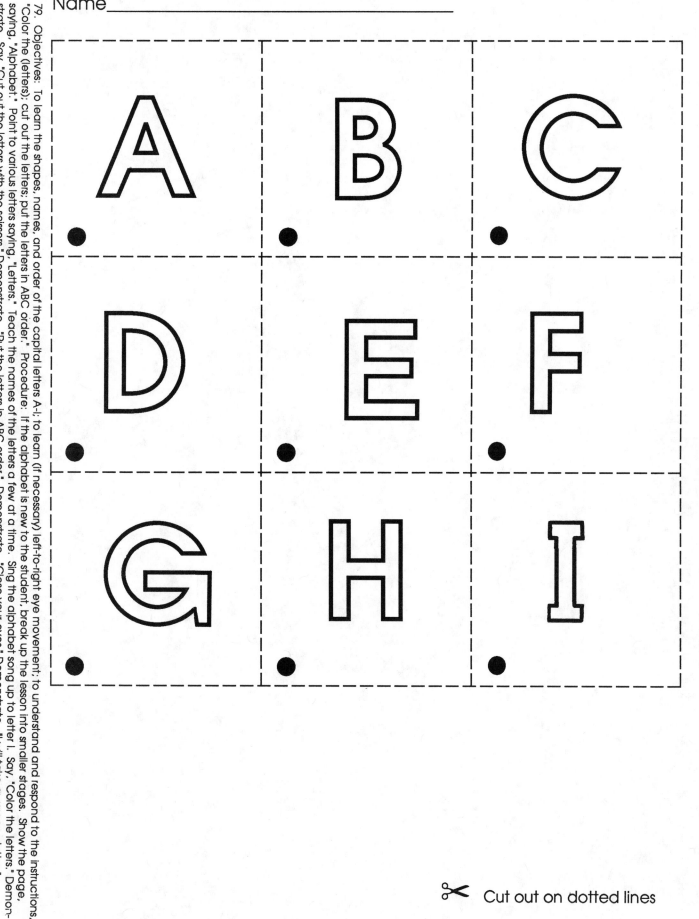

79. Objectives: To learn the shapes, names, and order of the capital letters A-I; to learn (if necessary) left-to-right eye movement; to understand and respond to the instructions, "Color the (letters); cut out the letters; put the letters in ABC order." Procedure: If the alphabet is new to the student, break up the lesson into smaller stages. Show the page, saying, "Alphabet." Point to various letters saying, "Letters." Teach the names of the letters a few at a time. Sing the alphabet song up to letter I. Say, "Color the letters." Demon-strate. Say, "Cut out the letters with the scissors." Demonstrate. "Put the letters in ABC order." Demonstrate. "Close your eyes." Demonstrate. "I will take away one letter." Remove a letter. "Open your eyes. What letter is missing?"

© ELIZABETH CLAIRE 1990

✂ Cut out on dotted lines

Name_____

✂ Cut out on dotted lines

Name_____

83. Objectives: To learn the shapes, names and order of the letters S-Z. Procedure: Review letters A-R and teach the names of the new letters. Sing the alphabet song.

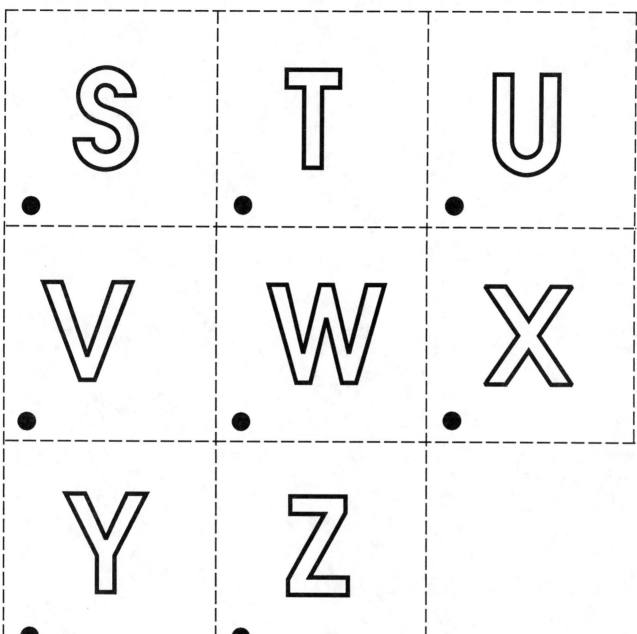

✂ Cut out on dotted lines

Name_____

85. Objectives: To learn the shapes and names of the small letters a–i; to contrast small and capital letters. Procedure: Point to the letters and say, "Small letters." Point to the letters from the previous lesson and say, "Capital letters." Point to the student's name and show that the first letter is a capital letter and the other letters are small letters. Sing the alphabet song. Say "Color the small letters." Say, "Cut out the letters with the scissors. Put the letters in ABC order."

© ELIZABETH CLAIRE 1990

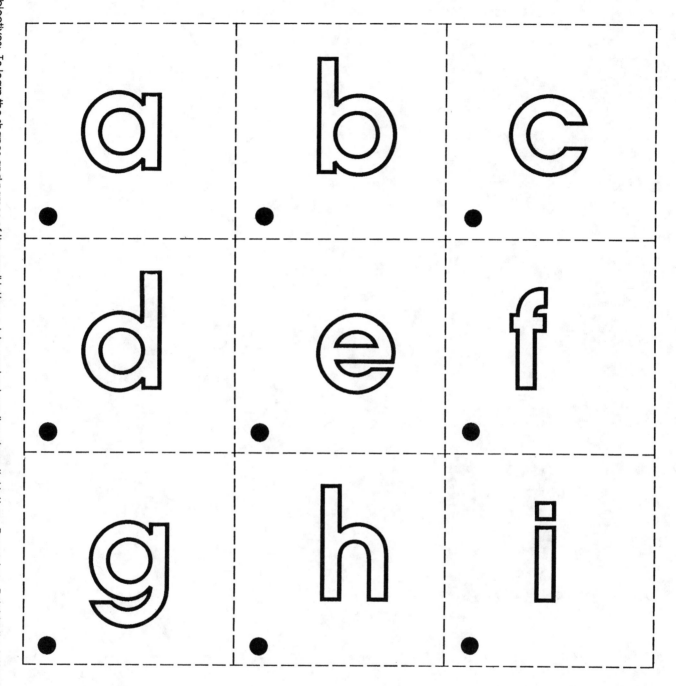

✂ Cut out on dotted lines

Name_____

87. Objectives: To learn the shapes and names of the small letters j-r; to learn the word word and reinforce left to right eye movements. Procedure: Review small letters a-i and teach the new letters. Sing the alphabet song. Say, "Find the letters g,i,r,l. This is a word. This word is girl. You are (not) a girl. Find the letters p,e,n. This is a word. This word is pen. Here is a pen." Continue with me, am, not, I, man, pencil, chair, ear, hand.

© ELIZABETH CLAIRE 1990

✂ Cut out on dotted lines

Page 87

s t u

v w x

y z

89. Objective: To learn the shapes and names of the small letters, s-z. Procedure: Review the letters a-r and teach the new letters. Sing the alphabet song. Say, "Find the letters b, o, y," and so on. Continue with cat, you, mouth, father, crayon, desk, and other words that the student already knows. Restrict this to words that use each letter only once. © ELIZABETH CLAIRE 1990

✂ Cut out on dotted lines

What is it ?

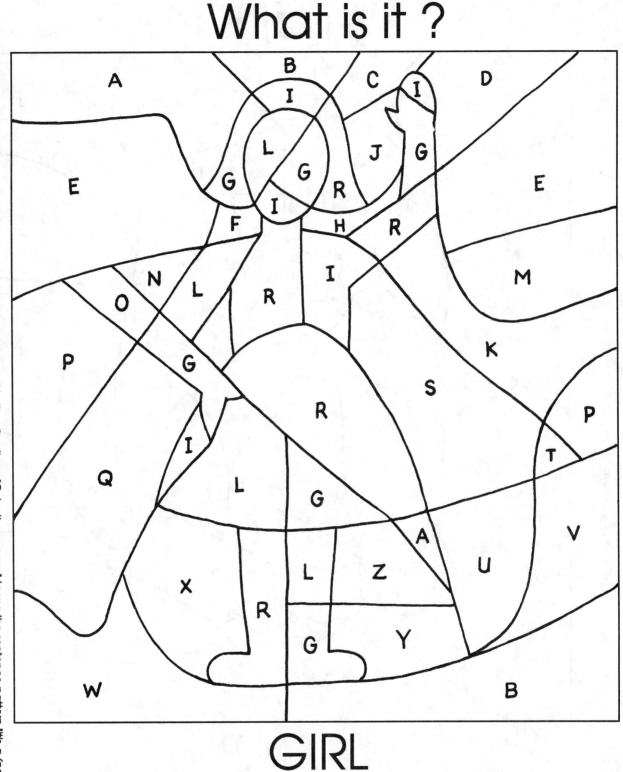

GIRL

Color the spaces that have the letters G , I , R , or L in them.

91. Objectives: To reinforce recognition of capital letters; to understand and respond to the directions. "Color the spaces;" to use the sentence pattern "It's a (noun)." Procedure: Say the word, girl, pointing to the word. Point to each letter and say its name: "G,I,R,L." Point to the spaces in the picture. Say, "Spaces. These are spaces. The spaces have letters in them." Point. This space has letter A. This space has letter B. Can you find a space with the letter G?" Hand the student a crayon or pencil. Say, "Color the spaces that have the letters I, R, or L in them." Demonstrate. "Good. Now color the spaces that have the letter G in them." When complete, ask, "What is it? It's a girl." © ELIZABETH CLAIRE 1990

What is it ?

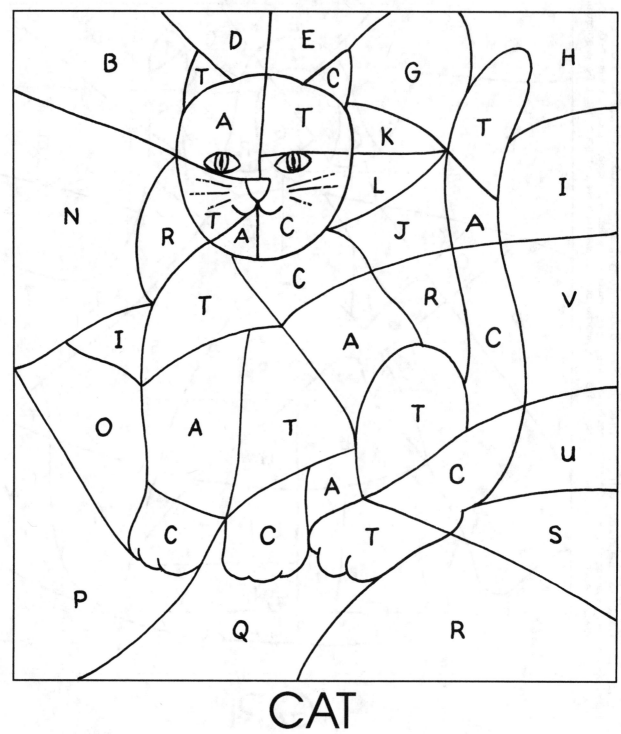

CAT

Color the spaces that have the letters
C , A , or T in them.

92. Objectives: To reinforce recognition of capital letters; to reinforce the words space and letter. Procedure: Say, "Can you find the spaces with the letter C or A or T in them? Color the spaces." When the student has completed the picture, say, "What is it? It's a cat."

© ELIZABETH CLAIRE 1990

What is it ?

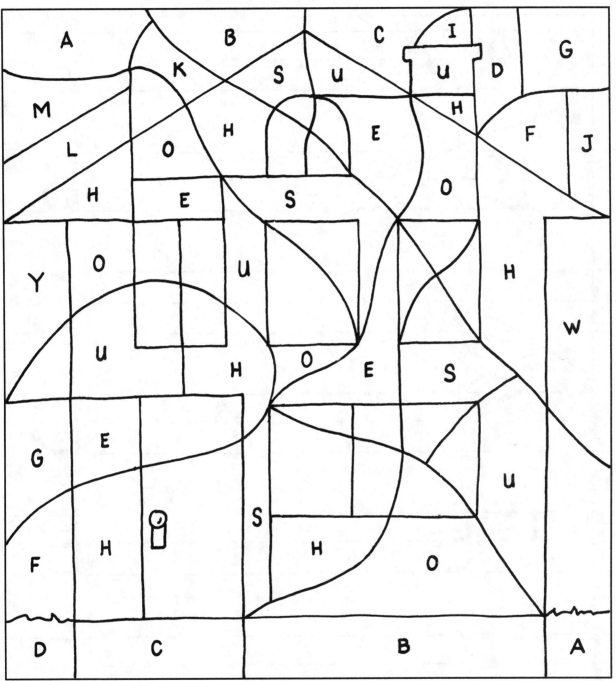

HOUSE

Color the spaces that have the letters
H O U S or E in them.

93. Objective: To reinforce recognition of capital letters Procedure: Say, "Can you find the spaces with the letters H,O,U,S,E in them? Color the spaces." When the student has completed the picture say, "What is it? It's a house."
© ELIZABETH CLAIRE 1990

Write the capital letters.

/ /\ /\ /\   A

| B B   B

C   C

| D   D

| F E   E

| F F   F

C G G   G

94-97. Objectives: To learn the order of strokes in writing capital letters; to practice writing; to reinforce alphabetical order. Procedure: Review the names of the letters, and review the alphabet song. Say "Write the letter A. Begin here at the dot. One, down, two, down, three, across." Point out the arrows and the number showing the order of the strokes. Say "Write the letter A three times." Observe as the student writes the letters to be sure the order of the strokes is understood.

© ELIZABETH CLAIRE 1990

Name_____

Write the capital letters.

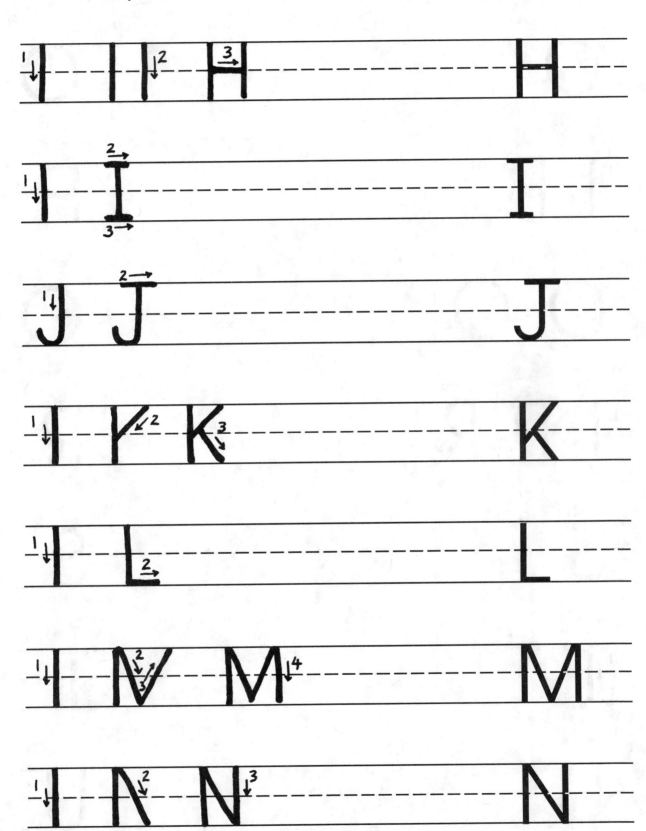

Name_____

Write the capital letters.

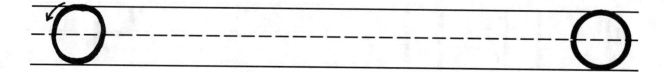

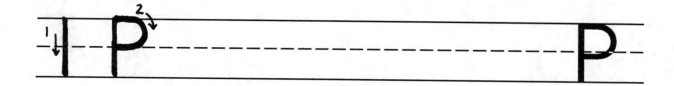

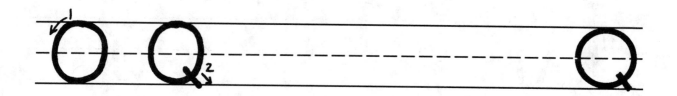

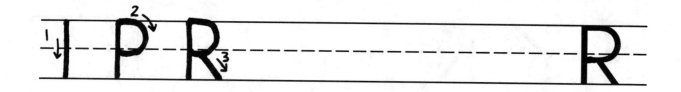

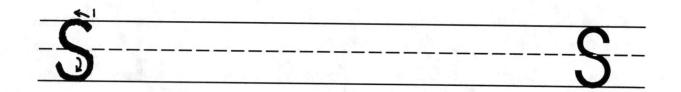

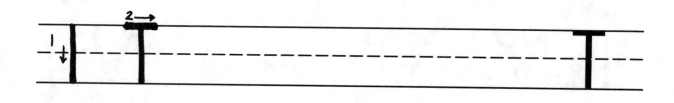

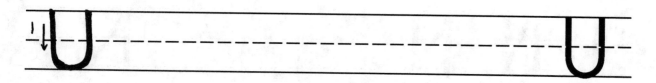

Page 96

Name_____

Write the capital letters.

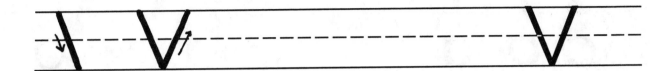

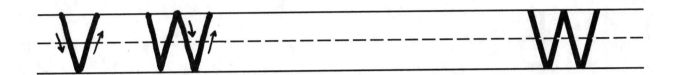

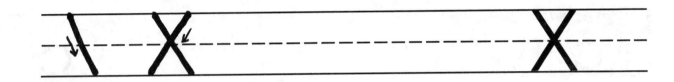

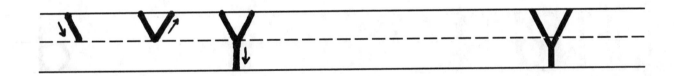

98-101. Objectives: To learn the order of strokes in writing small letters; to practice writing; to reinforce alphabetical order. Use the same procedure you used on pages 94-97. © ELIZABETH CLAIRE 1990

Name_____

Write the small letters.

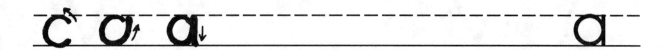

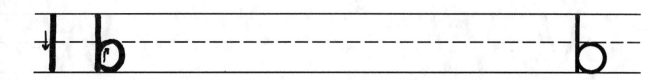

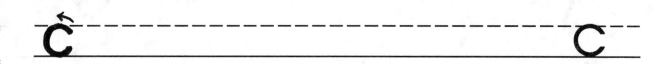

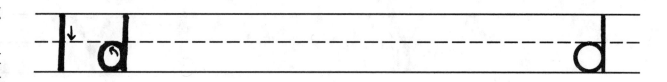

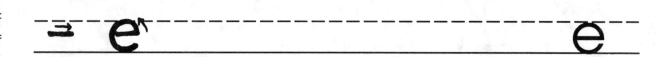

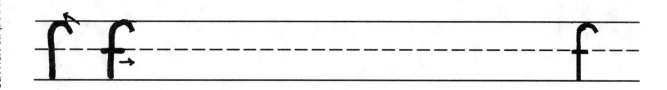

Name_____

Write the small letters.

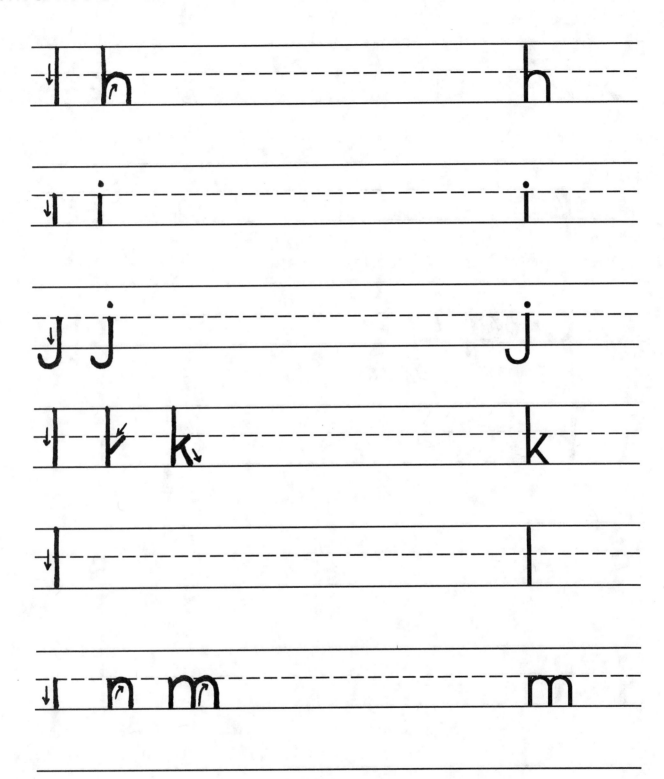

Write the small letters.

o   o

p   p

c o q q   q

r   r

s   s

t t   t

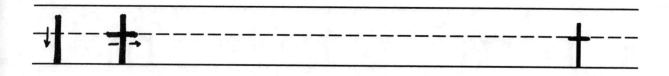

u u   u

Write the small letters.

v   V

w   W

x   X   X

y   y   y

z   Z

Draw a line from A to B to C etc.

A B C D E F G H I J K L M N O P Q R S T U V W X Y Z

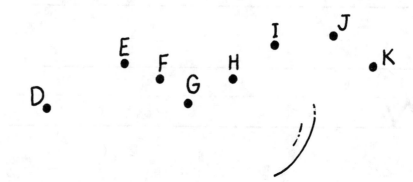

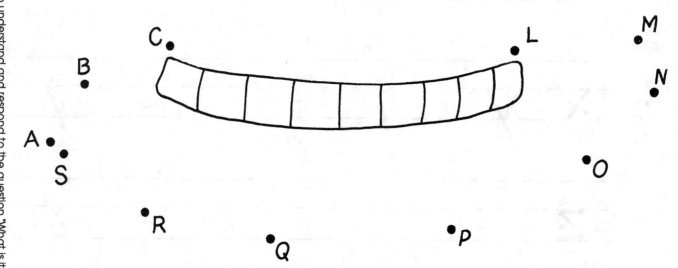

What is it ?

It's a _____.

102. Objectives: To reinforce alphabetical order, and recognition of capital letters; to understand and respond to the question "What is it?" with "I don't know." Procedure: Say, "What is it?" Shrug your shoulders and look perplexed. Model "I don't know," and have the student repeat this several times in answer to the question. Then say, "Draw a line from A to B to C." When the student has completed the picture, say, "What is it? I know. It's a hat." © ELIZABETH CLAIRE 1990

What is it ?

Draw a line from a. to b. to c. etc.

abcdefghijklmnopqrstuvwxyz

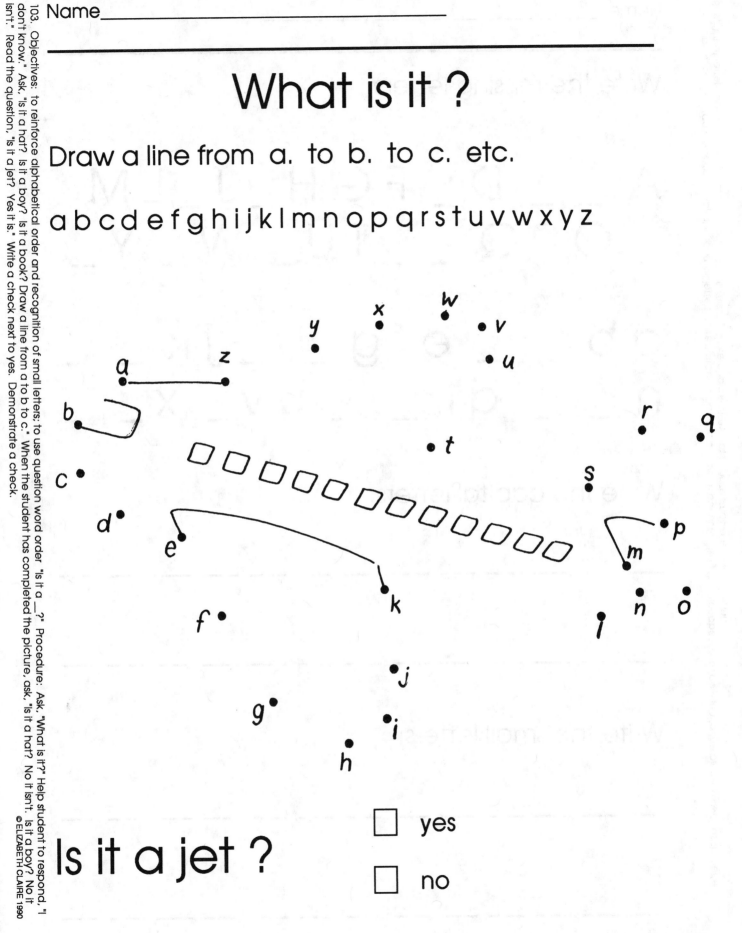

103. Objectives: to reinforce alphabetical order and recognition of small letters; to use question word order "Is it a ___?" Procedure: Ask, "What is it?" Help student to respond, "I don't know." Ask, "Is it a hat? Is it a book? Draw a line from a to b to c." When the student has completed the picture, ask, "Is it a hat? No it isn't. Is it a boy? No it isn't. Isn't." Read the question, "Is it a jet? Yes it is." Write a check next to yes. Demonstrate a check.
© ELIZABETH CLAIRE 1990

Is it a jet ?

□ yes

□ no

Name_____

_____

Write the missing letters.

A _ _ D _ F G H _ J _ L M

_ O P Q _ _ T U _ W _ Y _

a b _ _ e f g _ _ j k _ _

n _ _ q r _ _ u v _ x _ _

Write the capital letters:

— — — — — — — — — — — —

— — — — — — — — — — — —

Write the small letters:

— — — — — — — — — — — —

— — — — — — — — — — — —

104. Objective: To practice writing capital and small letters; to reinforce alphabetical order. Procedure: Sing the alphabet song, pointing to the blanks as well as the letters. Say, "What letters are missing? Write the letters that are missing. Write capital letters here. Write small letters here." Point.

© ELIZABETH CLAIRE 1990